Their Abstract Thoughts

Nefissa Bedri

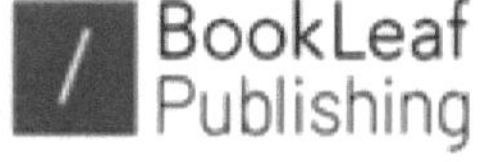

Presentation by *BookLeaf Publishing*

Web: www.bookleafpub.com

E-mail: info@bookleafpub.com

ISBN : 9789357611510

First edition 2021

DEDICATION

To all those who believed in me when I didn't,
my parents and those close friends, my siblings,
and those gems that are my people...

ACKNOWLEDGEMENT

I'd like to acknowledge BookLeaf Publishing for helping me achieve a long time dream of mine. A shoutout to Brooklyn White for creating this amazing book cover for me. My parents for always believing in me, my brothers and my friends who've always been there to pick me up when I felt like I was tumbling down, and I'd like to acknowledge myself for actually taking a step forward.

That woman

They took away her honour, they stripped her
dignity off,
They laughed at her words and sent her away
with a scoff.
They took her neck and broke it, so she always
looked at the ground,
They told her to keep her mouth shut, they made
sure her talents she never found.
They took her hands and feet and chained her to
the wall,
They then took her chained figure and pushed
her with her hands tied back so she couldn't
break her fall.
She fell face first and her jaw cracked, she felt
her head slam as blood trickled down her face,
There was no one to stand up for her case,
They then picked her up and told her she was
broken and she would stay that way,
They got her auctioned off and sold her to
anyone who would pay.
She was told to obey and she was told to bend
low she was told to never speak back,
But the woman never gave in, she never left her
track.
Her spirit is fire, it will soon ignite,

Be careful with her, she'll burn you down with
all her might.

His cage

His limbs were broken, his expression cracked and bare,
Invisible forces caging his lungs, stripping them of air.
His soul bruised and naked, welcoming each stare,
Those elegant movements now stumbles, that beauty no longer fair,
He was dead yet living, the worst way to be,
He couldn't feel nor hear nor see,
He was stranded alone somewhere in the dark,
Their arrows of judgements truly hit their mark but some part of him struggled to live and he forced into his lungs air,
His soul no longer open to each and every stare
They didn't matter, the only thing that mattered is he,
No one was going to imprison him, he was born free.

All the little things...

She found happiness in all the little things,
The little gifts that life sometimes brings,
The sunset, the smell of flowers, the cool breeze
of the wind hitting her face,
The sound of laughter, the feeling of a warm
embrace,
The smell of books, the sound of a tricking
stream,
They made her smile, trivial as they may seem.
The sharp scent of mint and the soft one of
jasmine
the smile on her mother's face , and the playful
glint in her father's eyes,
the steam wafting from freshly baked bread and
the smell of ground coffee
The burst of flavour of different types of spice
She found solace in places that most wouldn't
think of twice...

They call it Age

Age is but a number,
Your body a battle scar,
It's the heart that truly matters,
It determines how young you are.

Pain

So raw, pierces through us,
Makes us feel so fragile and hurt, not easy to
discuss,
We fear it, we relive it, we succumb to it ,
It breaks us or makes us, and shape us into what
we are ,
We all felt it, in different ways, yes, but we all
did so far,
It isn't easy to rub it off
It's not something that can be made fun of , not
something passed with a scoff,
She endured it in different ways ,
Family back lashes , friendship stabs and
lovelorn days,
She carved designs onto her skin to make that
raw hurt feeling reflect through her skin ,
She was afraid to let anyone in ,
He banged the door and punched the wall
He felt dejected and useless in the world, he was
ready to fall
He had no purpose in his eyes, yet he created
one for himself,
He had no one to look up to, he hasn't yet
checked the top shelf ,

The hurt and envy, the raw feeling inside was
killing them both
They still fought though , for they had less to
loose and more to gain,
For to them, it wasn't a stranger, they were used
to Pain.

And so she cut...

All she saw was chaos
all she heard were screams
all she felt was agony
Those thoughts in her head were louder than all
those outside
so to shut everything out and focus on
something- one thing alone- she cut.
To let her emotional pain turn physical... she cut.
She felt the darkness bleed out along with the
dripping blood...and so she cut.
She let herself forget that her body was the most
sacred temple
let herself forget that she was so much more than
where she was
or what she went through
let all her values and principles slip
she let go of what she was meant to be, what she
is, and what she was... and so she cut.

His spirit never died…

The arrow was fired ,
It cut through the air ,
It embedded itself in his chest, the wind
brushing past his tangled, dirty hair ,
His eyes grew wide and his lips were sealed, his
nostrils flared
As his body registered the pain,
His knees buckled and his fists uncurled ,
But he didn't completely fall yet, he heard the
arrow being fired once again, it hit the spot next
to the one before
His eyes closed and his lips parted, he inhaled
sharply, his body felt sore
His eyes fluttered open as he stared at his doom,
the third arrow hit him square in the chest, and
with that one blow he came tumbling down as
blood leaked out from those bruised lips
He heard a voice ringing out " He's dead . The
great warrior has fallen, never to rise again."
They weren't aware that he left his footsteps , he
realized .
For with every fallen warrior ,

another will rise .

The queen

She stared up ahead ,
She was full of potential, she really was, the
potential she constantly fed ,
She had a world full of possiblities , the
possibilities that she never spoke about
Her goals she sought ,
Her battles she bravely fought
She was humble the way most weren't gifted to
be
She had that gift most failed to see .
A positive attribute they claimed she had
The praise she graciously took without a
boasting word
That humbility she wore around her like a cloak
It was the key to the many possibilities, the key
that fit into the lock .

The dreaded body image

She just wants to be beautiful
She just wants them to think she is great
She just wants to decorate and predict her fate
It isn't for her to decide
To nature, she must abide
Alhough she wishes she could
She cuts down her calorie intake, decreases her
food
She tells herself she'd feel good once she hits her
goal
She starves herself and tells herself she's no
good, turning her soul black like coal
She fake smiles to show that she's okay
She lies to herself each and every day
She doesn't notice but she's actually killing
herself
Breaking her demons free and choking her
strengths
She tells herself she's ugly and seeks refuge in
friends
But it doesn't work that way.

If only she knew that she was leading herself
astray
She's beautiful, holds a beauty past what eyes
can see
She's the perfect version of who she can be .

Grief

Came unplanned an unknown visitor
It knocked on the door with a grim aura about, a
death claimer
The knocking didn't cease when they refused to
open the door
For it got more urgent, cracked through the floor
The unknown visitor was hooded and cloaked
They didn't know how to chase it away for the
fear encased their bodies, harshly it enveloped
The wind was silent trickling past the figure's
mane
For who would dare question it's existence, a
source of bane
It sent them creepy hollow stares, they were
unable to track
When they looked into its eyes the sockets of
death looked back
It robbed them off their cheery attitude and their
carefree smiles
It locked them in their own doors, standing in
the way ,blocking them from view letting them
face their own trials
The visitor still didn't leave
For this cloaked hooded figure was indeed
known as Grief .

You offered me your hand

"I remember vividly," she started, her voice cracked. She cleared her throat and started over." I remember vividly. I was in so much pain and you offered me your hand. You stretched it out in front of me with a scared look in your eyes. It was the first time someone ever offered me their hand before I even hinted that I needed someone, something to hold onto..." her voice trailed off into the silent night . When she turned to look at him, her eyes were wide, filled with wonder and mystery, they held an excited yet vulnerable glint to them . She smiled .

Broken dreams

She sat up straight, staring at the wall
Feeling afraid, afraid to fall,
Hope she did not have
Comfort she sought and will always crave
She knew she had dug her own grave
And so she questioned why she still fought
Each lies hopelessly bought, each excuse she
sought.
Her life wasn't how she'd pictured it
She was taught to shut up, act pretty and just sit
"Don't embarrass us, you're representing your
kin", they said, they let her wound and scar her
own skin,
But what was she, pointless those efforts were
When those she thought truly understood her
turned their backs on her.

Be that girl

Dear beautiful human,
You don't have to wake up at five and eat
smoothie bowls every day
You don't have to always look what seems to be
kept together and stylish as they say
You don't have to have a fixed schedule and go
on runs day by day
You don't have to always take insta-worthy
pictures with all the perfect angles and the
lighting
You don't have to have the best set up to work,
and the fanciest handwriting
You can be that girl without going through
extreme extents,
You can be her in your own way,
so get up at the time that makes you feel the best
and the most productive
Smile and laugh a lot, let those tears out when
you need to
Do what feels right for you
Surround yourself with people that prompt you
to be the best version of yourself
Work hard and chase those dreams, be
spontaneous and unpredictable

Dear girl, you don't have to compare your body
to all the other girls,
be you, you'll still be that girl
It's okay if you don't know what you want right
now, try different things
Experience all the joy that living life your way
brings
Widen your perspective, educate yourself
Don't waste away your day just because you feel
like you'd do it some other time
Build your empire, write down those ideas and
please rest when you have to it is not a crime,
My dear, live today like it was your last day,
buckle up and always remind yourself that
you're a warrior queen, and you are that girl.

His storm

She knows he's exhausted, she knows that he
just wants to dig a hole up and stay there
She knows that he thinks this world is so cold,
so unfair
She knows that he's terrified yet he's so brave, he
tries to hold on, to which string he does not
know
Every single day his pain seems to grow
She wants to reach out help him out of this
terrible cracking storm
But this isn't her storm , it's his and it's taken a
horrible form,
Even though it isn't hers she feels the blood
gushing out of his wounds
She sees the way he's breaking apart while all
she could do is call out
"Stay strong, my dear warrior." she yells with
her firm voice , she knows he'll understand, she
knows he'll still fight ,
"He'll survive ," she says to herself ", but first
he's going to destroy what already exist so he
could build a better him ."

Mine full of treasures untold

He was a mine full of undiscovered treasures
and it was hard to get through,
He didn't open up easily, he'd give everyone a
hard time too.
He'd lock himself in and never let them see,
How childish and fun, naive and sweet he could
be.
He'd throw on the tough facade and blend into
the wall,
He never failed to keep the mask on, he never let
himself fall.
But that mine isn't going to stay closed and
collecting dust forever more,
He'll eventually learn that he's enough after all.

Death will not do them apart

She stared into space
clutching at her chest, as if rubbing off the pain
in her heart, all of it, every trace,
A single tear tumbled on her cheek,
she felt her pain swarming in her forcing her to
close her eyes, forbidding her to take a single
peek.
Maybe this pain was short-lived and temporary,
Although she knew the pain of losing someone
close to her heart was etched onto it
permanently.
She held the photograph of him in one hand,
staring at his handsome face for he was gone and
would never stand.
She screamed out in pain,
Her thoughts driving madly through her brain.
It was too much to bear,
tipping the pain away wasn't not as easy as
wiping off a tear.
She looks around the room she one painted,

with him laughing and talking beside her, for
now it felt tainted.
For she lost all comfort that she sought,
Maybe, just maybe a little hope remained,
although it was absurd, she hopelessly bought...

Years later there she stood again in the same
room,
The room where she thought she met her
absolute doom.
But she has moved on,
Although she still loved him with all her heart
and she still felt the pain in every bone.
She knew he wanted her to live her life,
and for her dreams and goals to strive.
But she will always remember him and reserve a
place in her heart,
Because she still loved him, no matter the
distance and time, life and death will not do
them apart.

Solis

She admired the sun,
when everyone else wrote poetry about the
moon and the stars
she admired the sun,
A sole source of energy and light
The sun gave the moon its beauty,
she felt more like the sun than the moon,
lighting up every room she entered, her presence
always making things easier,
Her laughter contagious and her energy
unmatched,
her stubbornness and her fiery personality,
she will always be more like the sun than the
moon,
and so she admired the sun.

Possibility

That random smile that she received from the stranger on the street made her wonder if after all the world wasn't such a bad place to be...

Those scars

They said that they defined the fact that we
survived
They tell stories , a chance that we've been
deprived
They outline our bodies, and stand out proud .
They stand bold and hold their ground
They look gruesome and signify our struggle
Maybe they started with long bruises and a
bloody swollen knuckle
We hide them yet they show
They hold a story that they have yet to know
We survived yet we have them
We fought and we got them
We hid yet they came out
They are part of us, they are etched onto our skin
They reach our souls and lodge themselves in
Oh yes, they are beautiful in their own way
Cause those scars of ours will always stay.

No

26

Maybe things would've been different if she said no...

They're just words...

Words fight when she picks her pen up,
they fight to be the ones written on the paper.
It starts with a thought and then those words,
they start creating a crowd
And then it's like a gush of emotions one
tumbling after the other,
racing against each other...
And the words that win, they bleed through the
paper, their blood gushes black and blue,
purple and red at times
They never stop bleeding
over and over they bleed, scaring the pages,
print after print.
They tell a story, those words do.
They speak volumes about their wounds and
their fight, their fight to get on that page, to
anyone who reads them.
They're phenomenal those words...
They're art, poetry, and literature, they are
stories
yet some say they're just words...